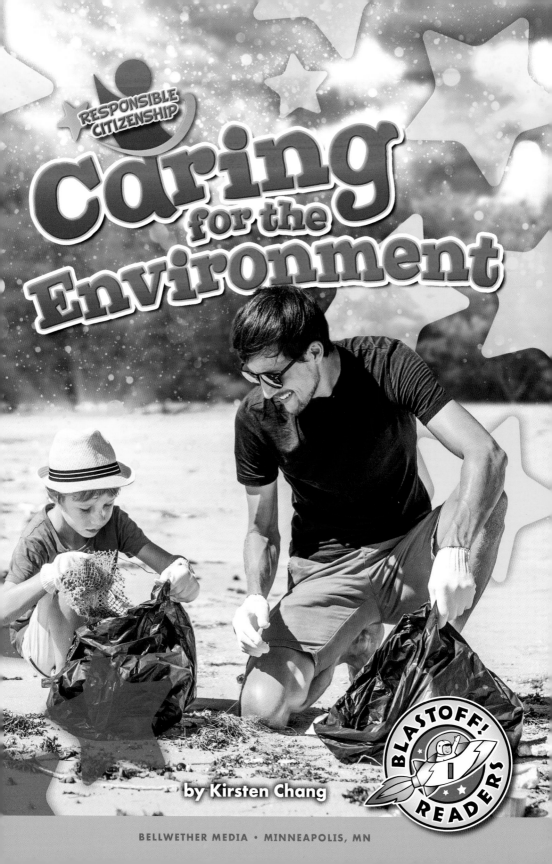

RESPONSIBLE CITIZENSHIP

Caring for the Environment

by Kirsten Chang

BLASTOFF! READERS

BELLWETHER MEDIA • MINNEAPOLIS, MN

Blastoff! Readers are carefully developed by literacy experts to build reading stamina and move students toward fluency by combining standards-based content with developmentally appropriate text.

 Level 1 provides the most support through repetition of high-frequency words, light text, predictable sentence patterns, and strong visual support.

 Level 2 offers early readers a bit more challenge through varied sentences, increased text load, and text-supportive special features.

 Level 3 advances early-fluent readers toward fluency through increased text load, less reliance on photos, advancing concepts, longer sentences, and more complex special features.

★ **Blastoff! Universe**

Reading Level

Grade **K**

Grades **1–3**

Grade **4**

This edition first published in 2022 by Bellwether Media, Inc.

No part of this publication may be reproduced in whole or in part without written permission of the publisher. For information regarding permission, write to Bellwether Media, Inc., Attention: Permissions Department, 6012 Blue Circle Drive, Minnetonka, MN 55343.

LC record for Caring for the Environment available at http://lccn.loc.gov/2021016554

Text copyright © 2022 by Bellwether Media, Inc. BLASTOFF! READERS and associated logos are trademarks and/or registered trademarks of Bellwether Media, Inc.

Editor: Kieran Downs   Designer: Brittany McIntosh

Printed in the United States of America, North Mankato, MN.

Table of Contents

Go Green!

Sam picks up trash.
He helps keep
the earth clean
and healthy!

4

How Do We Care for the Environment?

The world is full of land, water, air, plants, and animals. These make our **environment**.

We must care for the environment. We can pick up **litter**. We can plant trees.

litter

We can **reduce** what we use. We can buy things that can be used more than once.

reusable
water bottle

Some things can be **reused** instead of thrown away.

reusing trash
for art

We can **recycle**
some things
we cannot
use anymore.

Why Is Caring for the Environment Important?

We need the environment. But trash hurts the environment.

With/Without

clean
environment

dirty
environment

We must take care of
the environment.
This helps people,
plants, and animals
stay healthy.

We care for the environment because we love our world!

Question

Why do you think caring for the environment is important?

Glossary

environment

the land, water, air, plants, and animals around us

reduce

to make less waste by using less of something

litter

trash left on the ground

reused

used again

recycle

to make something usable again

To Learn More

AT THE LIBRARY

Boone, Mary. *Recycle It!* North Mankato, Minn.: Capstone Press, 2020.

Linde, Barbara M. *Celebrating Earth Day.* New York, N.Y.: Gareth Stevens Publishing, 2020.

Rustad, Martha E. H. *I Can Reduce Waste.* North Mankato, Minn.: Edge Books, 2019.

ON THE WEB

FACTSURFER

Factsurfer.com gives you a safe, fun way to find more information.

1. Go to www.factsurfer.com.

2. Enter "caring for the environment" into the search box and click 🔍.

3. Select your book cover to see a list of related content.

Index

The images in this book are reproduced through the courtesy of: Elizaveta Galitckaia, front cover; Monkey Business Images, pp. 4-5, 10-11; Sergei25, pp. 6-7; wavebreakmedia, pp. 8-9, 18-19; KaliAntye, pp. 12-13; Rawpixel.com, pp. 14-15; Fotos593, pp. 16-17; aboutsung, p. 17 (left); Photodigitaal.nl, p. 17 (right); Dmytro Zinkevych, pp. 20-21; cpaulfell, p. 22 (environment); SvRud, p. 22 (litter); Teresa Kasprzycka, p. 22 (recycle); StratfordProductions, p. 22 (reduce); The Childhood, p. 22 (reused).